SOUTHEAST ASIAN ASIAN FOOD AND DRINK

Christine Osborne

The Bookwright Press
New York · 1989

FOOD AND DRINK

British Food and Drink
Caribbean Food and Drink
Chinese Food and Drink
French Food and Drink
German Food and Drink
Greek Food and Drink
Indian Food and Drink
Italian Food and Drink

Japanese Food and Drink
Jewish Food and Drink
Mexican Food and Drink
Middle Eastern Food and Drink
North American Food and Drink
Russian Food and Drink
Southeast Asian Food and Drink
Spanish Food and Drink

First published in the
United States in 1989 by
The Bookwright Press
387 Park Avenue South
New York, NY 10016

First published in 1988 by
Wayland (Publishers) Limited
61 Western Road, Hove
East Sussex BN3 1JD, England

Typeset by DP Press, Sevenoaks
Printed in Italy by G. Canale & C.S.p.A., Turin

Library of Congress Cataloging-in-Publication Data

Osborne, Christine
  Southeast Asian food and drink / by Christine Osborne.
    p. cm. — (Food and drink)
  Bibliography: p.
  Includes index.
    Summary: Introduces the cooking and food habits of Southeast Asia, including such recipes as prawn soup and fried rice, and provides brief information on the people, agriculture, and festive occasions of the area.
    ISBN 0–531–18234–7
    1. Cookery, Southeast Asian — Juvenile literature. 2. Beverages — Asia. Southeastern — Juvenile literature. 3. Asia, Southeastern — Social life and customs — Juvenile literature. (1. Cookery, Southeast Asian. 2. Asia, Southeastern — Social life and customs.)
  I. Title. II. Series.
  TX724.5.S68083 1989   88–5959
  394.1'0959 — dc 19   CIP

Cover *People on the island of Bali bearing pyramids of fruits and flowers that are to be given as temple offerings.*

Contents

Southeast Asia and its people

The area known as Southeast Asia originally referred to all of the countries of the western Pacific lying between the southeast corner of the Asian landmass and northern Australia: Vietnam, Cambodia, Laos, Burma, Thailand, Malaysia, Singapore and the islands of the Indonesian archipelago and the Philippines.

In 1967, a regional association of countries known as ASEAN (Association of Southeast Asian Nations) was formed; it includes Thailand and the Malay peninsula, Singapore, Indonesia and the Philippines. They were joined in 1984 by the small, oil-rich Sultanate of Brunei. Now this area is officially recognized as Southeast Asia. The six member states enjoy a similar lifestyle with common food and drink. Their combined population exceeds 280 million.

Lying roughly between latitudes 20°N and 10°S, the area experiences high temperatures and a heavy,

Paddy-fields are typical scenery in Southeast Asia.

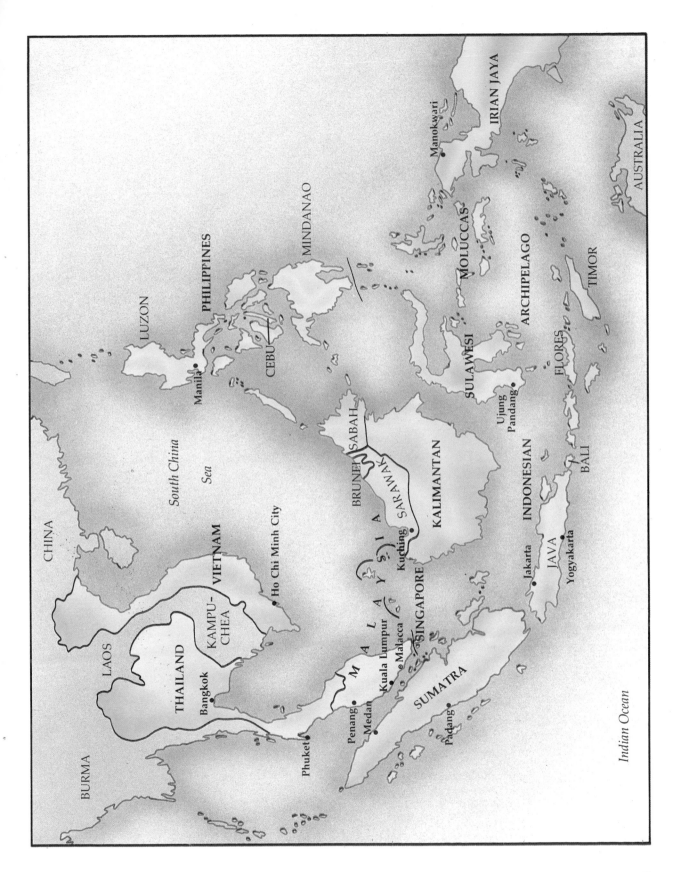

annual monsoon rainfall. Volcanoes are a characteristic of several islands in Indonesia and the Philippines. The highest peak is the majestic Mt. Kota Kinabulu in the eastern Malaysian state of Sabah. Where land has not been cleared for farming, mining and urbanization, the natural vegetation is jungle.

Buffaloes are traditional work animals in Southeast Asia. In the background of this picture you can see a volcano. Volcanoes are characteristic of many islands in Indonesia and the Philippines.

Human remains found on the island of Java indicate the existence of primitive man in Southeast Asia some 500,000 years ago. Tools discovered on the Korat plateau of northeast Thailand also indicate the existence of a rural community dated around 4000 BC.

Tribes of Tibeto-Burmese stock still inhabit the Chiang Mai hill tracts in Thailand, while other nomadic tribes roam the border area with Laos. Although they are now influenced by Thai culture, they retain their own traditions. This is equally true of the forest dwellers in Sarawak, Sabah and Kalimantan on the island of Borneo. Primitive tribes also inhabit the central highlands of Luzon in the Philippines. Tribes in Irian Jaya still follow a Stone Age culture.

Vietnam has a Chinese population of more than 500,000 living mainly in the south of the country.

Its ASEAN neighbors all have sizable Chinese communities. The business expertise of the Chinese is frequently a cause of local resentment.

Singapore is multiracial. Among its population of 2.5 million are Chinese, Indians and Malays. Chinese who intermarried with the native Malays are known as Straits Chinese, or Peranakans.

The inhabitants of Southeast Asia communicate in a variety of different languages. The main ones are Vietnamese, Thai, *bahasa Malaysia* and *bahasa Indonesia* and Tagalog, or Filipino. Singapore has four official languages: Chinese (Mandarin), Malay, Tamil and English, which is spoken by all educated people in Southeast Asia. Hundreds of different languages and thousands of different dialects are spoken by the various tribes.

Islam, Buddhism and, in the Philippines, Christianity are the main religions in Southeast Asia. There are also Hindu and Sikh minorities, mainly in Malaysia and Singapore. The remote tribes still practice animism, or spiritualism.

The region has a long history of disputes, ranging from the days when wars between the Thais, Laotians and Burmese were fought on elephants up to the twentieth-century struggle to unify Vietnam. The rich trade potential attracted European interest in the area in the early sixteenth century. By the nineteenth century, Southeast Asia had been divided up among the British, French, Spanish and Dutch. Portugal also controlled Timor, in Indonesia.

Vietnam became part of French Indochina; Britain administered Malaya and Singapore; and, following Spain's defeat in the Spanish-American War in 1898, the Philippines was controlled by the United States. All but the most inaccessible parts of Batavia (as the Dutch called Indonesia) had been colonized by the 1930s. The Kingdom of Siam (now Thailand) alone escaped colonization.

In 1942, Japan invaded Southeast Asia. Following the Japanese surrender to the Allies in 1945, Indonesia became independent. The Philippines followed suit in 1946, Malaya in 1957 and Singapore in 1959. In 1954 an agreement made between France and the Communist Vietminh divided Vietnam in two. After years of bitter fighting

A mosque in Malaysia. More than half the total population of Southeast Asia are Muslims.

involving American and Australian forces, the country was eventually unified under the Communist north in 1976.

The economies of the Southeast Asian countries vary according to the different levels of development. Vietnam has been set back after years of conflict, but the ASEAN countries produce, among other things, 95 percent of the world's hemp, 85 percent of rubber, 80 percent of palm oil, 67 percent of tin, and 60 percent of copper. The region is mainly agrarian, but inroads are being made by industry and manufacturing. Singapore is an exception, importing most of its food requirements, but it is South-

Western influences can be seen in the big cities, from Victorian buildings to highrise office blocks such as these in the background of the picture taken in Kuala Lumpur, Malaysia.

east Asia's leading commercial and communications center. Brunei and Indonesia are major oil and gas producers.

Western trends are evident in all but the most remote villages. The most obvious changes are highrise office buildings, department stores and supermarkets. But despite all the new international restaurants, there remain thousands of typical food stalls serving the same food Southeast Asians have been eating for centuries.

Growing the food

Rice is the main crop grown in Southeast Asia – Indonesia is the world's biggest producer. There are many different types of rice: lowland, upland, swamp, dwarf and floating rice. The spectacular terraces associated with rice-growing in this part of the world were built by the Ifugao tribe in the central cordillera of Luzon, in the Philippines. The rice terraces are watered by a complex irrigation system and rise more than 1,000 m (3,280 ft) from the valley floor. They are often referred to as "the eighth wonder of the world." Soaring step-terraces are also found in East Java. Rice cultivation in Vietnam is mainly carried out in the Mekong Delta, while the alluvial central plain is the rice bowl of Thailand.

Rice is the staple food of Southeast Asia. This woman is winnowing the rice.

Preparing for a new crop involves flooding the paddy fields in order to soften the soil, which is then plowed, traditionally by water buffalo. The seedlings, which are planted 10-12 cm (4-5 in) apart and are constantly underwater, mature in four to six months. Most areas average two harvests a year. Several weeks before the harvest, the fields are drained and fish are netted. Everyone then helps to cut the crop, although threshing is usually a woman's work. In some countries goddesses are associated with rice farming. The Thais place offerings to *Mae Phosop* in small temples on the edge of the paddy field in the hope that the gesture will produce a good harvest.

Rice is the staff of life in Southeast Asia. Long-grain is preferred, short-grain rice being used in desserts and confections.

Integrated farming, combining rice-growing, poultry-raising and fish-farming, is a very old tradition that enables a farmer to get

Cooking rice

The ideal measure is one teacup of rice per two persons. The rice should be thoroughly washed until clean. Place it in a saucepan and fill with cold water to an inch above the level of the rice. Add a pinch of salt and boil for 10 minutes, leaving the lid loose. When the water is absorbed and steam vents appear in the grains, put the lid on tightly and cook for 15 minutes on a low heat. Keep the rice warm in its own steam before serving.

maximum returns from his land.

Ducks are allowed to wander in the paddy fields by day where they keep down pests in the crop. At night they are housed in a pen on stilts above a pond. Food falls through the floor and feeds the fish. Other fish swimming in the paddy fields are caught with nets as required. The Torajas of South Sulawesi cut a deep pond in the center of the field where the fish congregate as the water level falls.

Integrated farming is practiced mainly in Thailand, but it is becoming increasingly important where similar conditions occur elsewhere. Marine culture is practiced in Thailand and also in Singapore.

The Philippines and Thailand are major producers of coconuts; fresh milk from grated coconut is widely used in Southeast Asian cooking. In the Surat Thani province of Thailand, monkeys are trained to collect the nuts.

Other edible crops grown in Southeast Asia are root vegetables,

A man and his wife catching shrimp in the silvery Southeast Asian dawn.

Chicken simmered in coconut milk

You will need:

3–4 lb chicken
2 tablespoons of grated onion
2 red or green chilies, seeded and
  chopped
3 cloves of garlic, chopped
1 tablespoon of peanut butter
2 tablespoons of grated lemon rind
2 tablespoons of fish sauce (or shrimp
  paste)
1 teaspoon of black pepper
1 teaspoon of cumin
½ teaspoon of ground ginger
2 cups of canned coconut milk
⅓ cup of coconut cream
coriander leaves

What to do:

Place the chicken in a saucepan. (1) Blend the other ingredients except the last three to a paste. Thin with a little coconut milk, then stir in the remaining milk. (2) Pour over the chicken and simmer just below boiling point for 45 minutes, or until tender. Turn the chicken to cook it on all sides. Remove the chicken and keep warm while you stir the coconut cream into the sauce. Simmer the sauce without boiling it. (3) Divide the chicken into portions and cover with the sauce. (4) Garnish with freshly chopped coriander leaves and serve.

Serves 6.

soybeans, peanuts, sugarcane, coffee, cocoa, corn and tapioca. In some of the more arid islands of Indonesia, sago replaces rice as the staple diet of people and animals.

Many of the world's favorite spices come from Southeast Asia. Islands such as Ambon and Ternate in the Moluccas, Sumatra and the Banda Islands of Indonesia are historically associated with the spice trade. Malaysia is the world's largest exporter of pepper. The hot tastes of local foods and *sambals* (dips) come from chilies. There are a dozen different types of chilies that flourish in the hot tropical climate of Southeast Asia.

There is also an abundance of exotic fruits. Some grow wild like the rose apple and the jackfruit. Other fruits, such as mangoes,

Rambutans *on sale in a Southeast Asian market.*

Monkeys are taught how to pick coconuts in Thailand. A good monkey will pick 500 a day.

pineapples and papaws, must be cultivated. Large plantations are found in the Philippines and southern Thailand. Exotic local varieties are the purple-skinned *mangosteen*, the hairy red *rambutan*, the *selak* (which has a snake-like skin and a crisp, apple-like texture) and the spiky *durian* (distinguished by a strong odor and soft, yellow, custard-like flesh). The Thais are passionately fond of mangoes – the local mango season being awaited as eagerly as strawberry time in New England. Forty-one varieties of mangoes grow in the Philippines, the two most important being the *carabao* and *pico* (the first is named after the Asian water buffalo). The sweetest mangoes come from Luzon Island and the Visayas.

Selling the food

Getting all of the food to market is usually a complex business and may involve several different means of transportation. Inter-city buses play a major role but, in the early hours, trucks, trains, bicycles, *becaks* (human-powered tricycle

A floating market in Thailand. The vendors are usually women.

taxis), *bemos* (mini-buses), boats, *jeepneys* (taxi-jeeps, often U.S. army surplus) and pony carts are busy bringing produce to urban areas.

In remote districts, farmers may have a long trek to market on foot. On market day in Rantepao, in Toraja land, South Sulawesi, you can see people walking along the roads carrying trussed pigs and heavy bamboo poles with pails of foaming fermented rice wine. Carrying eggs, yams and wild bananas, tribes in Irian Jaya may take several days to reach the market site. By contrast, oysters seen in Phuket, a seaside resort in Thailand, arrive daily on Thai Airways from the Gulf of Siam.

Markets serve a practical purpose for locals, but they are also an attraction for visitors, and no two markets are the same. The most colorful are the floating markets in rural Thailand where boats laden with fruit and vegetables are paddled from door to door along the river. Traders take great pride in the appearance of their food: eggplants are polished a gleaming purple and chilies are laid out in geometric patterns. Most market vendors are women, although men are found in the meat and poultry sections – chopping, plucking and skinning. Selling food is a family effort for the Chinese who are always hard at work processing bean curd, shredding coconuts and slicing bamboo shoots.

Stalls selling food and drink are

A Filipino turo-turo *restaurant where you point at what you want, sit down and eat.*

inseparable from the market, while peddlers roam about advising shoppers of their wares. Shoppers can quench their thirst on a variety of fresh juices and satisfy their hunger on the endless choice of snacks. Popular items are tapioca cake, rice and prawn biscuits, *satays*, fried bananas and dried fish. *Turo-turos*, stalls where you point out what you fancy, are common in the Philippines. Tempting snacks are *lumpia* (egg rolls) or *lugao* (rice porridge) and *tocino* (strips of cured beef). Special dishes are sold during the hot season: connoisseurs in Thailand cannot wait to eat their first *khao chae* of the year. This is a cooling bowl of rice soaked in scented water topped with ice. Iced sugarcane juice and coffee are sold by vendors in the busy Ben Thanh market in Ho Chi Minh City (formerly Saigon). Malays like ABC, a coconut jelly and ice dish.

The nutritional value of food

Southeast Asian food is one of the healthiest diets available in the world. It uses plenty of raw food-stuffs such as salads and fruits. The brief method of stir-fry cooking does not rob vegetables of their natural goodness. Based only on

Natural foods – plenty of salads, seafood and vegetables – are a major part of the diet.

vegetable oils such as soybean and peanut, cooking oils are devoid of saturated fats. The custom of steaming food, in particular fish, is also a healthy way of cooking.

Southeast Asians are great fish-eaters. Fish is low in fat and it is mainly muscle tissue protein, which is more easily digested than the connective fiber in meats. Fish

is the best source of vitamins A, D and B complex. Low in sodium, it also contains valuable supplies of iron, phosphorous and potassium.

Natural raw food such as salads, fruits and coconut milk, together with the high fiber content of rice, makes Southeast Asian food easy to digest. Some of the cooking ingredients, such as tamarind, aid absorption and place a minimum strain on digestive organs. Chilies,

Widely used in cooking, chilies are believed to lower the blood pressure, in spite of their hot taste!

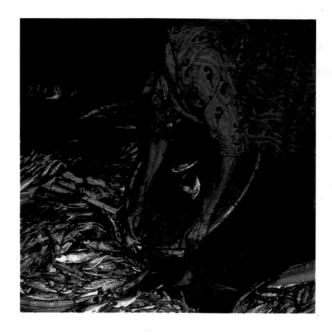

People in Southeast Asia are great eaters of fish, an ideal source of vitamins A, D and B.

which are widely used in Southeast Asian cooking, are believed to lower the blood pressure. People are usually slim as a result of this diet. The incidence of heart disease is lower than with the high protein and carbohydrate diet of the West.

Raw juices such as sugarcane, coconut milk, pineapple, pomegranate, tamarind and soybean milk are popular beverages full of natural goodness. Local wines, which are brewed from fermented rice and coconut milk, are relatively low in alcohol. Herbal drinks remain popular, especially among the Chinese communities. Tea and coffee are drunk in moderation although, as with modern supermarkets, coffee shops are a growing trend in cities such as Singapore, Manila and Bangkok.

16

Cooking equipment and methods

Most cooking in Southeast Asia is done on an open, charcoal stove. Food is either grilled or barbecued, simmered, steamed or stir-fried. Other local methods of preparing foods are smoking and salting. Fish and shrimp are fermented to obtain a pungent sauce or paste.

A Western-style gas stove can cope with most recipes, but an essential piece of equipment for the popular stir-fry cooking method is a *wok*. This is a shallow, concave pan that balances on a light metal frame. Its shape permits the precise amount of evaporation needed to cook vegetables slightly under-done (see page 45).

Most recipes require spices to be ground into a paste. This is done using a pestle and mortar. The Straits Chinese community in Malacca and Singapore claim to

One of the many ways of preparing food – salting and drying fish.

Chili-hot marinated pork

You will need:

1 lb of pork, cut into small cubes
2-3 fresh red or green chilies, seeded and chopped
3 cloves of garlic, crushed
¼–½ teaspoon of ginger root, grated
2 teaspoons of brown sugar
1 teaspoon of shrimp paste (available in specialty stores)
1 teaspoon of salt
2 tablespoons of peanut oil
1 medium onion, diced
1 teaspoon of grated lemon peel, or a stalk of lemon-grass
Juice of a lemon
2 cups of canned coconut milk, or

What to do:

(1) Mix the chilies, garlic, ginger, sugar, salt and shrimp paste in a bowl. Add the pork, mix well together and allow to marinate for one hour. (2) Heat the oil in a *wok* and fry the onion until golden. Add the pork and stir-fry over medium heat for about 3 minutes. Add the lemon-grass, or peel, the lemon juice and coconut milk to the *wok*. (3) Turn the pork pieces well in this mixture, bring to the simmering point and cook until the pork is tender, about 40-50 minutes. Serves 4.

judge a good cook by his or her ability to pound a good *rempeh* (a paste made from ground spices and herbs). In a Western home, an electric blender or food processor can be used to make the paste. If it becomes necessary to add liquid to the paste, use whatever the food is being cooked in. Otherwise use a small amount of chicken stock.

Other useful items are a cleaver, strong scissors, a sharp kitchen knife and a curved vegetable knife. Skewers are required for *satay* (see page 25) and tongs for lifting food.

Experts at cooking rice, the Filipinos use an earthenware pot lined with banana leaves to prevent sticking: thick-based saucepan does the same thing. Kitchen foil is a substitute for banana leaves when steaming food.

Chinese-style bowls with large ·dishes for rice make a dinner look authentic. Soups are best served in a tureen: local restaurants keep them hot by simmering them over a charcoal burner.

A spoon and fork are usually used for eating. The Vietnamese and Chinese use chopsticks, Malays and Indonesians commonly eat with the right hand.

Almost everything for cooking Southeast Asian food is seen in this picture of a stall in Singapore. How many things can you identify?

Traditional foods

Southeast Asian food is basically similar wherever you go in the region. All the countries have a mutual love of rice, with seafood and poultry being the most popular dishes. Common ingredients are herbs and spices (especially chilies and lemon-grass) and coconut milk. Filipino food is slightly different from that of its ASEAN neighbors, having been greatly influenced by the Spanish occupation and the use of a lot of pork. The Vietnamese, Thais and Chinese communities also eat pork, which is forbidden to the Muslims of Indonesia and Malaysia. At first glance, local food looks the same, but close study reveals subtle regional variations.

Although Thailand itself was never colonized, the food has been influenced by trading links with Indonesia, China and India. These foreign tastes have been absorbed into what is now a uniquely Thai cuisine.

Thai food is aromatic, spicy, salty, sweet and sour, and, at times, extremely hot from the use of chilies. Chilies and lemon-grass give the traditional seafood soup, *tom yam kung*, its pungent taste.

Thais in particular enjoy cooking in coconut milk. This fresh, white milk is obtained from grated coconut flesh after it has been soaked in warm water and squeezed through cheesecloth. It is also available in cans. Fish is often steamed in it, and coconut milk also forms the basis of chicken and duck curries. *Nieo mamuang* (sliced mangoes, "sticky rice" and coconut cream) is a popular dessert.

Som tam is a classic Thai salad made from lettuce, sliced papaw, shrimp and peanuts served with

Workers will have breakfast at a stall like this one outside Bangkok's central market.

Tom yam kung (prawn soup with lemon-grass)

You will need:

20 prawns (or shrimp)
4 cups of light stock
3 shallots, finely chopped
2 tomatoes, skinned and sliced
2 stalks of lemon-grass, pounded
2 tablespoons of fish sauce
1 teaspoon of ginger, freshly grated
6 kaffir lime leaves (use lemon as a
    substitute)
2-3 tablespoons of lemon juice
2 small red or green chilies
Coriander leaves, chopped

What to do:

(1) Shell the prawns or shrimp leaving the tails on. Heat the stock, shallots, ginger and fish sauce in a saucepan and simmer gently for 5 minutes. (2) Add the prawns and tomatoes and cook until the prawns turn pink. Add the kaffir lime leaves, chilies and lemon-grass and cook for a further 10 minutes. Season with salt and pepper according to taste. (3) Finally garnish with chopped coriander leaves. Serves 4.

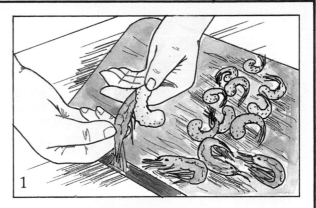

barbecued chicken and rice. Side dips are common. So is *nom pla*, a pungent liquid extracted from fermented seafood. *Nom pla* is the Thai equivalent of soy sauce, or *nuoc mam* in Vietnam.

A meal always includes soup, either fish or poultry, salad, a vegetable dish and a bowl of rice.

The people of southern Thailand like fiery dishes, often based on seafood, whereas the northerners prefer milder cooking. For a quick snack, rural Thais lightly cook raw vegetables, which they serve with *nam prik* (a dip based on *nom pla* and chilies) and grilled fish.

Breakfast for Thai city workers is

often soup or noodles bought from market vendors and street stalls. Lunch of rice and curry is also eaten at a simple sidewalk restaurant.

At home, or in a better class restaurant, the appearance of the food is important. Soups arrive with carved cucumber flowers floating on the surface, and lotus-shaped carrot-buds and tomato rosettes may decorate a bowl of rice. In addition to learning how to cook, Thai chefs are taught the art of fruit and vegetable carving. Court cuisine, a refined art once practiced only by women of the royal household, features minute portions of exquisitely decorated food. It is likened to an Asian-style

Thai chefs are taught the art of carving fruits and vegetables. This carved melon gourd is stuffed with seafood.

nouvelle cuisine.

Indonesian food is comprised of an infinite number of tastes and textures. Since Indonesia is made up of so many different islands, it is not surprising there is such variety. At different times in history, local food has been influenced by Indians, Arabs, Chinese and also by the Dutch who devised the famous rice table, or *rijsttafel*, of their favorite appetizers. *Rijsttafel* is practically unheard of in Indonesia today: only the Oasis Restaurant in Jakarta serves anything similar to

22

this ethnic smorgasbord.

The common ingredients in Indonesian recipes are chilies, lemon-grass, kaffir lime leaves, tamarind, coconut milk and, in particular, spices. Like its Southeast Asian neighbors, Indonesia makes use of *trasi* (*blanchan*, or fermented shrimp paste).

The best known cuisines are from central Java and Padang, in western Sumatra. The former is sweet as well as spicy, the latter is known for its hot, spicy food. A classic Padang dish is the extremely hot *rendang*, which should be made from buffalo meat and simmered for three to four hours in coconut milk.

Simple to prepare, *nasi goreng*, or fried rice, is synonymous with eating in Indonesia.

Poor people might eat only a plate of plain rice in a day, but despite Indonesia's vast and growing population, no one is starving. Stuffed *ikan* (fish) and *soto* (soup), are both traditional. There are said to be as many recipes for *soto ajam* (rice and chicken soup) as there are cooks in Indonesia!

A properly balanced meal includes rice served with four to six dishes consisting of soup, poultry, meat, fish, egg and vegetables, which may be fried, stewed or

Some Indonesian dishes including satays, rice, stuffed fish and shrimp crackers.

Nasi goreng

You will need:
1½ cups of cold, cooked rice
1 lb of ground rump steak
a handful of raw shrimp, shelled
1-2 fresh red or green chilies
1 medium onion, chopped
1 clove of garlic
½ teaspoon of *trasi* (shrimp paste)
1 tablespoon of soy sauce
2 eggs
oil
salt
To garnish: onion flakes, cucumber,
  tomato and a fried egg.

What to do:
Beat the eggs with a pinch of salt. (1)
Heat a little oil and cook the eggs to a
thin omelet. Remove, cool and cut into
strips. (2) Using a pestle and mortar
grind together the chilies, onion, garlic
and *trasi*. Heat a tablespoon of oil in a
wok (*wajan* in Indonesian) and fry this
mixture until soft. (3) Add the steak and
shrimp and stir-fry until cooked.

Now add the rice and mix well. Add
the soy sauce and turn thoroughly until
the rice grains are evenly coated. (4)
Serve on a dish garnished with the strips
of omelet, fried onion flakes and
chopped celery. Garnish with a fried egg
and sliced tomatoes.
Serves 2.

steamed. *Gado-gado* are lightly cooked vegetables including potatoes, carrots and beansprouts, along with soybean curd and hard-boiled eggs, doused with peanut sauce spiked with *trasi*, garlic and coconut milk.

Prawn crackers, or *krupak*, are popular. *Sambals* (chili-hot dips) are always served with a meal. If you should burn your mouth on chili dips in Southeast Asia, ask for plain rice – drinking cold water makes it worse. As in Thailand, a meal commonly ends with fruit, such as melon, papaw, pineapple or *selak* – depending on the season.

While Malay food is less varied, it closely resembles Indonesian and

Gado-gado *(bottom left) with a bowl of* sambal, *a hot chili dip, (top left).*

Indian cooking. Penang has a reputation for the best food, especially seafood. The states of Kelantan and Perak also have specialties such as *rendang tok*, a dry, dark, rich-colored beef curry.

The spicy, hot curries in Malay cooking were introduced by Tamil immigrants. Other, moister curries using *ghee* and coconut milk are a North Indian influence. *Satays* (skewered beef or chicken) grilled over an open fire are the symbol of Malay cooking. They are usually dipped in a sauce made with peanuts and eaten with rice cake.

Malays eat a selection of dishes similar to those of the Thais and Indonesians, with about four to five courses including meat (never pork) followed by fruit. Some famous dishes are *inche kabin* (chicken marinated in coconut milk and chilies, deep fried and served with a mustard and soy sauce), *otak-otak* (spicy, boned fish) and *sambal udang* (curried prawns). As in Indonesia, *sambals* are popular.

Filipino food is a mixture of Spanish, Chinese and Malay. At times it can be exotic, at other times bland. A local appetite for rice is the basic thing in common with other Southeast Asian nations. Some popular dishes are *adobo*, a method of braising pork that has been cured in garlic and vinegar. *Adobo* may be dark and savory in Manila, but elsewhere crisp. Many dishes have Spanish origins, such as *calamares fritos* (fried squid) and *paella* (savory rice). Cooked everywhere, yet considered the most exotic dish by foreigners, is *dinguan*. This is pork, including the organs, stewed in seasoned pig's blood.

Various regions contribute to the national cuisine. Pampanga is known for chewy, garlic-flavored *tapas* of beef, pork and venison.

Hot peanut sauce

You will need:

2 tablespoons of oil
2-3 finely-diced green or red chilies
2 cloves of garlic, crushed
1 small onion, finely diced
1 teaspoon of curry powder
½ lb of peanuts, fried in 1 tablespoon of oil
1 cup of water
1 tablespoon of brown sugar
1 teaspoon of grated lemon-grass (or lemon peel)
salt and pepper to taste

What to do:

(1) Heat the oil in a pan and add the chilies, garlic, onion and curry powder. Sauté until the onion turns gold. (2) Add the remaining ingredients, stir well and bring to a gentle boil. Reduce the heat and continue stirring until the sauce becomes thick and rich.

Ilocano cooks in North Luzon prepare a dish based on fermented fish and wild greens. *Ginataan* (a mixture of yams, jackfruit, tapioca and bananas cooked in coconut milk) from South Luzon, is also a favorite.

Bananas range from tiny, sweet "senoritas" to the chunky *saba* used in cooking. With mangoes, they are the most popular fruits.

In addition to authentic Chinese cooking, Singapore provides a microcosm of all Southeast Asian cooking, in particular Thai, Indonesian and Malay.

It shares with Malaysia, in particular the town of Malacca, a local type of cooking known as

Lechon (suckling pig) in Manila, the Philippines, being loaded into the back of a car to be taken to a restaurant.

Straits Chinese, or Peranakan. The Malay and Chinese influences have evolved an exotic cuisine based on ingredients from both countries.

The Chinese influence in Peranakan food is reflected in ingredients such as mushrooms, seaweed and the use of soy sauce. Peranakans also use coriander in their cooking, like the Thais, but their recipes are very complex using lots of pungent roots such as ginger and turmeric. Beancurd is popular. *Laksa* is a delicious traditional Peranakan soup based on a rich

27

Fried banana cakes

You will need:
4 large bananas, ripe enough to mash
2 teaspoons of brown sugar, to taste
2 tablespoons of flour
½ teaspoon of salt
oil for deep-frying

What to do:
(1) Peel and mash the bananas in a bowl until completely puréed, then add the sugar. Stir the flour and salt together and add little by little to the mixture, stirring well with a wooden spoon. Add water or more flour to obtain a consistency that will drop from the spoon. Cover the base of a pan with cooking oil and heat until sizzling. (2) Drop in a little of the mixture at a time and fry until the patties turn golden brown. Remove and drain on a kitchen towel. (3) Serve hot, or cold, dusted with brown sugar.

Safety note: Be very careful when cooking with oil. Hot oil burns. Ask an adult to help.

broth made from coconut milk and prawns and finished with noodles and beancurd. *Ayam siyow* (chicken in tamarind sauce) is another interesting Peranakan dish. *Chap Chye Nonya* is the Peranakan version of a Chinese vegetarian dish that includes a *rempeh*, (a mixture of ground chilies, shrimp paste, lemon-grass, coriander with other herbs and spices).

Fruit is unpopular at mealtimes. Instead, Chinese-style cakes and desserts based on rice, gelatine and coconut milk are preferred.

Coconut rice, or *nasi lemak*, is served with a variety of dishes as part of an elaborate feast or merely a snack. In Singapore, hawkers prepare small packages of the rice with a slice of cucumber, a few *ikan bilis* (dried fish) and some *sambal*. Inexpensive, they are wrapped in banana leaves, and the hawkers usually advertise their product to passers-by with the call, "*nasi lemak, nasi lemak.*"

In former times, Vietnamese food had a reputation second to none. In many ways it is very like Chinese food, but it is more fragrant and refined due to the subtle influence of neighboring Thailand. A hint of Malay cooking is also evident in

Peranakan cooking is a blend of Chinese and Malay cuisine. Laksa *soup is in the center of this picture.*

Fried oyster omelet

You will need:
About 10 oz of small oysters
⅓ cup of rice flour
⅔ cup of water
Salt to taste
6 eggs
3 spring onions
1 clove of garlic
1 small red chili
1 tablespoon of soy sauce
oil for cooking
Coriander leaves

What to do:
Mix together the flour, water and salt to make a batter and set aside. (1) Chop the onions, garlic and chili fine. Beat the eggs lightly in a bowl. (2) Heat a small amount of oil in a wide frying pan and when it is sizzling, pour in the batter and top with the beaten eggs. Sprinkle with the chopped onion and add the soy sauce. Cook rapidly, turning once. When the omelet is cooked, break it up with a spatula and shift to the edge of the pan. (3) In the center add the oysters, chopped garlic and chili and cook for 2-3 minutes, stirring continuously. (4) Finally mix together with the omelet and serve with side bowls of chili sauce and garnish with freshly chopped coriander leaves.
Serves 4.

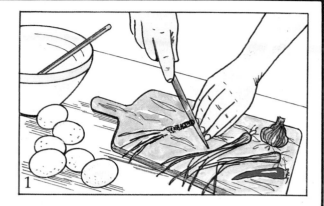

some of the spicier dishes.

Today's high prices and food shortages in Vietnam see many families struggling to keep up traditional standards. Even rice is expensive and the price of cooking oil is inflated beyond most people's means. Vegetables, which are fundamental to every meal, are often boiled instead of the usual stir-fry method. Central Vietnam is especially poor.

This being the case, a typical Vietnamese meal includes a clear soup, vegetables and a fish or poultry dish. Duck is more widely used than chicken. Pork or beef are common in dishes, usually braised

People often stop for a snack at a hawker's stall, like this one in Ho Chi Minh City, Vietnam.

with a mixture of beansprouts, mushrooms, spinach, mustard and greens. Frogs' legs are popular among rural communities where frogs are easily caught in the paddy fields. French influences are found in Vietnamese cooking, but this is not one. The Thais also eat frogs' legs. Long, crisp, French loaves are, however, eaten with soup for breakfast in Vietnam. When it is obtainable, iced coffee is very popular.

Breakfast is always soup, usually *pho* (made with rice or noodles).

Other popular items are *xoi*, or rice with mung beans, and rice pancakes with mung beansprouts and fish sauce. People stop to eat at hawkers' stalls on the way to work.

Lunch is usually light, and those who can may take a siesta. Dinner usually consists of five dishes, which vary according to what is available. On Sunday, a family tries

Seafood for sale in a Vietnamese market.

to have more elaborate dishes, such as seafood pancakes and grilled prawn balls.

Typical Vietnamese appetizers are fried sweet potato and prawn pie, chicken *satay*, shredded seaweed and grated scallops. Like their ASEAN neighbors, the Vietnamese are passionately fond of seafood. Eel soup is traditional, while *goi sua* is a colorful dish made from jellyfish. One of the best known Vietnamese appetizers is spring rolls whose basic ingredients are minced pork, beansprouts, carrots, shrimp and crab meat. *Nuoc mam*, a pungent fish sauce similar to the Thai *nom pla*, is used as a dip.

Sweet and sour prawns

You will need:
1–1½ lb of prawns (or shrimp)
2 tomatoes, sliced
1 large onion, sliced
1 small red chili, sliced
½ a cucumber, sliced
1 green pepper, sliced
2 tablespoons of sugar
6 tablespoons of tomato sauce
Chili sauce
Vinegar
Sesame oil
Cornstarch

What to do:
Heat some oil in a *wok* and stir-fry the prawns until they change color to pink. (1) Remove the prawns and add the cucumber, chili, pepper and onion. Stir-fry for abut 2-3 minutes. (2) To this add 6 tablespoons of tomato sauce, ½ teaspoon of cornstarch mixed in 5 tablespoons of water and stir-fry for about 20 seconds.

Add 2 tablespoons of sugar, a dash of sesame oil, 1 teaspoon of vinegar and salt to taste. (3) Place the prawns in the sauce and mix thoroughly for about one minute.
Serves 4.

Meals and customs

The amount and quality of food eaten depends on a family's economic status of which there are great extremes. On the one hand is Singapore where people eat well; on the other is Vietnam where for many a bowl of soup and rice must suffice. A cheap, sustaining snack found all over Southeast Asia is fried bananas.

Broadly speaking, a middle class family enjoys four to five courses in their main meal of the day – soup, poultry, fish or meat, salad and a vegetable dish. The order of eating varies somewhat: Thais tend to eat their soup throughout a meal, and the Chinese usually end with a soup to clear the palate.

Likewise, table habits are dependent on whether the family is rich or poor. The well-off pull up chairs to a Western-style dining table, although in typical Muslim tradition, Malays and Indonesians feel more comfortable eating off a

Malays and Indonesians are happy eating off a cloth on the floor. Hands are used for eating and are rinsed after the meal.

Chinese communities use chopsticks to eat. Note the small charcoal stove, center, keeping the food warm.

tablecloth spread on the floor.

The food is brought all at once, either by the mother and grandmother who have cooked it, or by a domestic servant. Elderly people are treated with respect in Southeast Asia and are served first, or are first to help themselves. In Indonesia it is the custom to begin a meal with the phrase *"selamat makan!"* meaning "good appetite!" It is also customary to leave a spoonful of rice on the plate as a mark of respect to Sri Dewi, the local goddess and patroness of rice.

Malays and Indonesians often eat with their hands, or, more correctly, with the right hand. In former times, the Thais also ate with their hands, people with aristocratic backgrounds extending their "pinkie" to display the family ring. Anna, the tutor of Rama V's children, is said to have introduced the idea of eating with a spoon and a fork. Today the spoon and fork are most widely used in Southeast Asia, the spoon acting as a fork, and

the fork as a "pusher." The people of the Vietnamese and Chinese communities use chopsticks.

Crockery is usually blue and white or the five color patterns of Chinese classic styles. The banana leaf has many uses other than wrapping foods for cooking – in the Philippines it is used as a plate on which food is served, or fashioned into "cups" to hold the food.

Different foods are taboo among the various religious groups found in Southeast Asia. Pork is forbidden to Muslims in Malaysia, Indonesia and the Philippines – stalls selling pork are even isolated from the rest of the market. The Hindu popu-

A Thai army officer, his wife and child bring food for a monk. The gesture is considered to be an honor.

lation, which is found mainly in Singapore, Malaysia and Bali, does not eat beef. Vegetarian dishes are common among the many Indian communities.

In Thailand it is an historic custom to look after the monks. Every morning the monks make a food round, and people fill their bowls with rice, fish or whatever the family may be eating. At dawn hundreds gather outside Bangkok's Marble Monastery where residents drive up with cars filled with food.

Drinks

The most traditional drinks are based on fresh fruit juices; some of the best are made by hawkers cranking juice out of ancient fruit-presses. Lime, sugarcane and mango juice are the most popular juices. Chilled coconut milk makes a cooling beverage and, when the liquid has been drunk, the shell is cracked and the soft white flesh can be scraped out as a snack.

Some of the more exotic fruits also make exciting drinks. Among them are star fruit, tamarind and a rather sour tasting lemon-like fruit called a *calamansis* in the Philippines. The Toraja *terong*, or tree tomato, is pressed into a frothy pink juice rivaled in flavor only by passion fruit juice.

Tea and coffee are not drunk much, although Western-style coffee shops are a growing trend. Bottled soft drinks are enjoyed by the young.

The older, rural generation, especially in Vietnam, Thailand and the Philippines, is partial to rice wine, which is made by fermenting rice for about six months. Palm wine is also made from fermenting the juice of coconuts.

Herbal drinks are enjoyed in Vietnam, Thailand and among the

Bottled cane juice for sale in Phetchaburi, a town in Thailand famous for its sweets and drinks.

various Chinese communities. Most are taken as a tonic to increase the strength and for their medicinal value. Many of the original formulas in Thailand are said to come from around Chiang Mai. Some examples are *khun polphat special*, which is taken as a remedy against pain and fatigue, and "tiger power," a potion against insomnia.

Southeast Asia is famous for excellent quality beer – *"Bintang"* in Indonesia, *"Tiger"* in Singapore and

Many farmers in Southeast Asia make rice wine, sold here by Torajas in South Sulawesi.

"San Miguel" in the Philippines are first-class brands. Tribes from the Ilokano regions of Luzon, in the Philippines, were growing sugarcane not only as a source of sugar but also for a fermented drink called *basi* as early as the seventeenth century. *Basi* is undistilled rum: *"Tanduay"* and *"Manila"* rum are exported worldwide.

Festive foods

Southeast Asia's multifaceted culture is enhanced by its many different religious festivals and other events.

Malaysia and Singapore, in particular, celebrate with feasts and pageantry marking the Chinese, Christian, Hindu, Sikh, Muslim and Buddhist New Years, as well as anniversaries such as the birthday of the Monkey God, the feast of Saint Peter, Easter and the Thimithi fire-walking festival.

For several weeks before New Year in Singapore, Chinatown is packed with people shopping for delicacies. Among these delicacies are oranges wrapped in gold paper, which are a sign of good luck. On New Year's Eve, the family and relatives gather for a big dinner where favorite foods such as braised abalone and black mushrooms are served.

Festive foods include a New Year cake, or *niangao*, made from brown sugar and sticky rice and *tang yuan*, which are rice balls stuffed with sesame seeds. Celebrations last for two days as younger members of the family visit their elders, receiving in return red packages of "lucky money," or *ang-pows*.

During the "open house," tidbits such as pineapple tarts, cookies, red and black melon seeds and strips of barbecued pork are offered to visitors. Chinese New Year is celebrated in a similar way by Chinese communities all over Southeast Asia.

Another important event for the Chinese is the "Double Fifth" (the fifth day of the fifth month of the Chinese lunar calendar) commemorating the suicide by drowning of the Chinese poet Ch'u Yuan in 3 BC. When people heard of his death, they threw rice dumplings into the

Spectacular pyramids of fruit are made as temple offerings on the Indonesian island of Bali.

river to prevent his body from being eaten by the fish. Today, steamed rice dumplings, called *chungs*, wrapped in banana leaves are cooked in his memory. The event is also celebrated in Singapore by a spectacular Dragon Boat Festival.

The Vietnamese also celebrate the Chinese Mooncake Festival that marks the anniversary of the overthrow of the Mongol rulers in China. Rich, round pastries filled with red bean and lotus-seed paste are exchanged on this day.

Tamil communities celebrate *Avani* with special offerings to Ganesh, the son of Lord Siva. In Malaysia a special sweet is placed before his statue along with twenty-one kinds of leaves, twenty-one varieties of flowers and twenty-one pieces of grass. Coconuts are smashed before the deity.

At Buddhist celebrations in Thailand, no special foods are cooked, although vendor's stalls outside the temples overflow with foods at festival time. *Macha Bucha* commemorates the time when thousands of monks gathered to hear Buddha preach. It is marked by a huge gathering of monks in Bangkok where people bring donations of food such as rice, noodles, salted fish and fruits.

At the Plowing Ceremony in Thailand, sacred cows are offered rice, grasses and water – their willingness to consume the gifts being indicative of the forthcoming season. The eastern Malay states celebrate the end of the harvest season by dancing and drinking rice wine. In Sarawak, the Dyaks mark the occasion by sacrificing a white cock.

The Torajas in Sulawesi have complex funeral ceremonies that involve the ritual sacrifice of buffalo, whose meat is cooked and shared among the villagers.

Muslims in Southeast Asia sacrifice an animal on the occasion of *Eid al-adha*, a sacrificial feast marking the end of the pilgrimage to Mecca.

Yogyakarta in East Java marks the Prophet's birthday with spectacular pageantry. *Grebeg Mulud*, as it is known, is preceded by a huge night bazaar selling all kinds of foodstuffs. The next day, huge ceremonial mounds of food are brought in a procession to the Grand Mosque where they are dismantled and distributed to the crowds. Also held on Bali are

A Chinese funeral in Manila. Food is placed on top of the tomb.

Boiled eggs on a Malay wedding table are a symbol of luck and fertility.

elaborate temple ceremonies where people make towering pyramids of flowers and fruits.

Christmas is a grand occasion in the Philippines, echoing the country's Spanish past. Candlelit tables are loaded with Spanish-types of dishes such as *galantinas* (stuffed chickens), roast suckling pig and rich desserts.

Special foods feature in many marriage ceremonies in Southeast Asia. Three days before a traditional Straits Chinese wedding, the groom accompanies twelve trays of wedding gifts to the bride's home. They include four bottles of brandy, a duck or chicken, bananas and half a pig. Beneath the marital bed is placed a bowl containing a lemon, a banana and a yam. The lemon symbolizes long life, the banana wealth and the yam fertility. Specially wrapped hard-boiled eggs to wish the couple many children are also distributed at weddings in Malaysia.

Weddings, birthdays, graduations and feast days (of which there are more than thirty) all call for feasting and celebration in the Philippines, and since Filipinos consider food as a common gift to be shared, a plate is never returned to its owner completely empty.

Southeast Asian Food Abroad

Chinese and Vietnamese are the best known Southeast Asian cuisines abroad. There is a thriving Chinatown in each of the major world cities, while small rural towns usually have a local Chinese restaurant.

The French, having been colonial rulers of Indochina, are the most familiar with Vietnamese food. Paris and Marseilles boast dozens of Vietnamese restaurants.

Vietnamese, numbering well over 75,000, make up the largest number of newly arrived immigrants in Australia. Many have settled in the Sydney suburb of Cabramatta, which is known locally as "Little Vietnam." As a result, a number of Vietnamese restaurants have opened.

Indonesian food is becoming increasingly popular abroad.

Indonesian rijsttafel *at the Bali Restaurant in Amsterdam, Holland.*

Holland is the center of Indonesian cooking in Europe. The Bali Restaurant in Amsterdam is internationally renowned for *rijsttafel*.

The *turo-turo* in its original, humble form has been brought to America by Filipino migrants and is found at numerous street fairs in major cities.

The increasing popularity of Thailand as a holiday destination has seen an increase in Thai restaurants. London has over thirty of them, although most serve "Chinese-style" food rather than authentic Thai cuisine.

Malay restaurants are not common outside Southeast Asia, although the famous *satay* is

Many of the vegetables popular in Southeast Asia can be found abroad, as in this Chinese supermarket in Soho, London.

featured on many Southeast Asian menus abroad.

The only place to eat typical Straits Chinese food is in Singapore itself. So far Peranakan cooking has not traveled beyond the tip of Southeast Asia.

Singapore is also the best place to sample all types of Southeast Asian food – in deluxe hotels or at simple food stalls.

In the United States, Chinese groceries and specialty stores sell most of the ingredients for cooking Southeast Asian food.

Herbs and spices

The following are some of the more common herbs and spices used in Southeast Asian cooking.

Bay leaf: used in soups, curries and as a garnish.

Cardamom: used to flavor curries in Malaysia.

Chilies: an ingredient in most recipes. The smallest are the hottest.

Citron or Kaffir lime: skin and leaves used for flavoring.

Coriander: widely used, especially in Indonesia and Malaysia. Leaves are a popular garnish in Thailand and the Peranakan community in Singapore.

Cloves: native to the Moluccas in Indonesia. Used in curries.

Cumin: mainly used to make a paste.

Garlic: used fresh or as oil. Oil and fried garlic can be stored in a jar. Garlic and vinegar are popular ingredients in Filipino cooking.

Ginger: widely used in cooking. Several varieties. Its edible flowers are batter-fried in Thailand.

Lemon-grass: a tall, fragrant, reed-like grass widely used as a flavoring. The stalk is close-packed like a tiny leek. Only the lower bulb is used.

Mace: outer covering of the nutmeg, native to the Banda islands in Indonesia. Used in making pastes for curries.

Mint: used as a flavoring and also as a vegetable.

Nutmeg: grated fresh for making curry pastes.

Pepper: black or white, widely used in cooking.

Sesame: tiny seeds, rich in protein, used as a flavoring.

Shallots: onion-like plant. An important ingredient in most Thai dishes.

Tamarind: sour fruit pods used as a flavoring in Indonesian and Malay cooking. The pulp is soaked in water, which is used as the flavoring agent.

Tempe: a fermented soybean product with a nutty taste added to other dishes in Indonesia; also fried and served by itself.

Turmeric: a member of the ginger family, but without the hot flavor. Provides the yellow color in curries, rice and vegetable dishes.

Glossary

Abalone Edible shellfish that have an ear-shaped shell.

Agrarian Relating to cultivated land.

Allies The countries that fought against Germany, Italy and Japan in World War II. The main allied powers were Britain and the Commonwealth countries, the United States, the USSR, France and Poland.

Alluvial Relating to a fine-textured, fertile soil consisting of silt, mud and sand deposited by flowing water.

Animism The attribution of life to inanimate objects. Spiritualism. Practiced by primitive tribes having close spiritual links with nature.

Archipelago A group of islands.

Aromatic Fragrant or spicy smelling.

Connoisseurs Knowledgeable judges (of food, drink, art, etc.)

Cordillera A series of parallel ranges of mountains.

Eid al-adha and **Eid al-fitr** The Muslim feasts signaling the end of the pilgrimage and the end of the fast month of Ramadan.

Fish sauce A thin, salty, translucent brown fluid made from liquid filtered from fermented fish, in particular from anchovies. It is available in specialty stores.

Ghee Butter that is free from impurities; clarified butter.

Grebeg Mulud The Prophet's birthday in Indonesia.

Hawkers People who travel from place to place selling goods.

Hemp A fibrous plant used for making ropes, etc.

Insomnia Inability to fall asleep or to enjoy uninterrupted sleep.

Microcosm A miniature representation of something.

Multifaceted Having many aspects.

Paddy field A field where rice is cultivated.

Rijsttafel Table of Indonesian *hors d'oeuvres* devised by the Dutch.

Shrimp paste A pungent ingredient used throughout Southeast Asia. Rich in Vitamin B, it is a major source of protein. Known as *kapi* (Thailand), *blachan* or *trasi* (Indonesia), *cencalok* (Malacca); available in specialty stores.

Tana Toraja The region in central South Sulawesi inhabited by the Torajas, a Christian tribe who practice traditional rites including the sacrifice of buffalo at funerals.

Tapas A Spanish word meaning tidbits. Small plates of food, usually eaten with a drink.

Turo-turos Restaurants and fast-food stalls in the Philippines that serve a great variety of home-style foods. The meaning is "to point out what you want."

Vietminh A Vietnamese organization that first fought the Japanese and then the French and the United States in order to achieve national independence.

Further reading

Betty Crocker's Cookbook for Boys and Girls. Western Publishers, 1984

Cooking the Vietnamese Way by Chi Nguyen and Judy M. Monroe. Lerner Publications, 1985

A Family in Thailand by P. Jacobsen & P. Kristensen. Bookwright Press, 1986

Follow the Sun: International Cookbook for Young People by Mary Deming and Joyce Haddard. Sun Scope, 1982

Let's Look Up Food from Many Lands by Beverly Birch. Silver, Burdett & Ginn, 1985

We Live in Indonesia by Chris Fairclough. Bookwright Press, 1986

We Live in Malaysia and Singapore by Jessie Wee. Bookwright Press, 1985

We Live in the Philippines by Gilda Cordero Fernando. Bookwright Press, 1986

Index

Acknowledgments

Christine Osborne wishes to thank the following for help with the preparation of this book: Philippine Airlines, national airline of the Philippines, member of the Chaine des Rotisseurs, the Department of Tourism in the Philippines, The Thai Tourism Authority, The Malaysian Tourism Development Corporation, The Department of Tourism of South Sulawesi (Indonesia), The hotels Mandarin and Marina Mandarin in Singapore, the Regent and Imperial hotels in Bangkok, The Oasis Restaurant in Manila and Yasmin Restaurant in Kuala Lumpur.

The publishers would like to thank the following for their permission to reproduce copyright pictures: Huchison Library 31, 32, Wayland Picture Library 14. **All other photographs were supplied by Christine Osborne.** The map on page 5 is by Thames Cartographic. All step-by-step recipe illustrations are by Juliette Nicholson.